EMERGING *from the*
SHADOWS

GREGOR SOUTHARD

WESTBOW
PRESS®
A DIVISION OF THOMAS NELSON
& ZONDERVAN

Scriptures taken from the Holy Bible, New International Version®, NIV®. Copyright © 1973, 1978, 1984, 2011 by Biblica, Inc.™ Used by permission of Zondervan. All rights reserved worldwide. www.zondervan.com The "NIV" and "New International Version" are trademarks registered in the United States Patent and Trademark Office by Biblica, Inc.™

WestBow Press books may be ordered through booksellers or by contacting:

WestBow Press
A Division of Thomas Nelson & Zondervan
1663 Liberty Drive
Bloomington, IN 47403
www.westbowpress.com
1 (866) 928-1240

Because of the dynamic nature of the Internet, any web addresses or links contained in this book may have changed since publication and may no longer be valid. The views expressed in this work are solely those of the author and do not necessarily reflect the views of the publisher, and the publisher hereby disclaims any responsibility for them.

Any people depicted in stock imagery provided by Getty Images are models, and such images are being used for illustrative purposes only. Certain stock imagery © Getty Images.

ISBN: 978-1-9736-2005-1 (sc)
ISBN: 978-1-9736-2007-5 (hc)
ISBN: 978-1-9736-2006-8 (e)

Library of Congress Control Number: 2018901935

Print information available on the last page.

WestBow Press rev. date: 3/26/2018

For more, visit: www.gregorsouthard.com, on
Facebook, Instagram, Pinterest, and Twitter.

TABLE OF CONTENTS

INTRODUCTION

You will, no doubt, find the formatting of this book a little different from the normal memoir. This book was born from my blog *Christianity Is A War,* written from May of 2012 through October of 2014. Instead of rewriting everything into longer, more traditional chapters, I decided to leave the blogs in their original form (albeit with much editing). My hope is that the reader will find some value in experiencing these moments much like I did, not in a traditional narrative, but in the moments that led to a single conclusion. What you will find is a man searching for what Christ called "abundant life." The quest ends up being a life transformed from years of bitterness and despair to peace in Jesus Christ.

That is what unfolds in these essays, culminating in "Emerging From The Shadows," which I decided to make the title of this collection. Along the way, you will find prayers of praise interspersed throughout this book. Here, I took a cue from St. Augustine's *Confessions* where at the beginning of many chapters, he offers up prayers of thanksgiving to God. I hope you find this book encouraging and useful.

"That's what happens when you're the nice guy."

A sort of random prologue to whatever comes next

A few years back, I was sitting in a familiar coffee house talking with a friend of mine when the conversation went from art, faith, and friends to the struggles we were facing. I don't remember most of the conversation, it was a few years ago after all, but I remember us talking about the uneasy feeling of being caught in the middle of a dark forest. We weren't "missing the forest for the trees," we were all too aware of the trees crowding in and around our lives, call them "the cares of the world" if you like, and our being tempted to run through that forest to try and out run or escape them. If that makes any sense.

Here I am, a few years later, sitting in a booth at the same coffeehouse in the expanded section. In a receding economy, my favorite haunt has figured it out. It has not only survived the storm, it has thrived. The continual buzz of coffee drinkers and organic salad eaters is the soundtrack of success and busyness. I'm happy for them, though I do miss the library feel it used to convey to those few who first discovered "the little coffeehouse that would."

What am I trying to do here? I'm not quite sure yet. Frustrated with the modern state of poetry, I set it aside over a year ago. Frustrated by the many factors that have contributed to a lack of opportunities for my books and screenplays, I quit writing all together. I'm not an Art-for-

Art's sake kind of guy. So, what am I trying to do here? I can't keep up with journals. My autobiography doesn't interest me, either. Yet, there seems to be a story in here somewhere.

It's not like I haven't tried. I wrote a pilot for a television series titled "What It's Like To Die" as a sort of comical autobiography of my life but it took on a life of its own despite the real life references to my experiences as a frustrated would be professional writer. I have started a legitimate autobiography, whatever that means, a few times that I want to call "I Am Daffy Duck" with little luck. I like the premise, though. Daffy is the quintessential "other guy." You know who I mean. You always hear people say things like "I love Bugs Bunny! And also Daffy." Or, "Taz, Marvin the Martian, the Tasmanian Devil, etc is my favorite, oh, and I like Daffy, too." That's what happens when you're the nice guy. Everyone's glad you're around but you're not the one they're seeking out at the party, as it were.

Still, while I want the t- shirt, I'm not concerned with that as an overarching theme or issue. I'm stuck in this forest, and I want out. And the more I run, the deeper in I seem to find myself. Maybe that's why I started writing my blog titled "Christianity Is A War." I will say, it was kind of exciting, or at least a little intriguing, to start a blog with a potentially controversial title without knowing where this was going to lead.

So, I sketched out a feeble, poorly written explanation of what the blog was going to be about and began to write. I did know, that as a Christian, this would not be an anti- Christian blog. Obviously. And it would not be pro- war, either. It ended up being what I should have expected it to be, musings on what was on my heart at that particular moment, how my faith infused how I approached and reacted to it, and whatever insight I thought came from the experience. Pretty much what I tried to do with my poems, stories, and songs.

So, here I am, outside my blog trying to figure out what I'm doing here. And come to think of it, you may be wondering the same thing about yourself. What in the world *are* we doing here? I mean, besides looking, straining for the good life, whatever we happen to think that is at any given point in our stories. Let's start with what we do know about life; it's a journey, and every journey has a story. There it is, a story to tell. Now we're back in my territory, or comfort zone, you might say.

Where to begin? I was born into a pretty typical American family and led a pretty typical Middle Class American early life. Yeah, that as a story doesn't interest me either, even though I'm grateful for it. I could use the Daffy Duck metaphor to spice things up a little bit but then this would be little more than an autobiography at best or a low budget comedy at worst.

It does get a bit more interesting in my early twenties as I began my studies at Kansas University. Not just because attending KU was such a great experience but because it was also during this time that I made an adult decision to follow Christ, or "J" as I oftentimes refer to him in my blogs (see the appendix, "J's Coming: Look Busy" at the back of the book for an explanation).

My decision launched the happiest decade, I mean years, of my life. The next four years were a time filled with a new found innocence and grace that allowed me to grow into a more mature man with a much sunnier outlook on life.

Those days ended eventually, of course, worn away as real life and daily decisions began to form my adult life. Thus, the happy, grace filled life was replaced with bad decisions and the ensuing consequences. Maybe there's a movie in there somewhere but no decisive ending (as of yet). The journey, with all its bumps, bruises, and moments of comic relief continued and continues.

The blogs in this collection are presented in the order they were written. You will see early on that I was borderline obsessed with finding "abundant life" in the midst of trying to find a full time job and reconcile what had happened to me. These blogs represent the process of walking through what felt like what King David calls "the valley of the shadow of death (Psalm 23:4)" and emerging from a place of bitterness and despair to a place of "peace which surpasses our understanding, (Phil 4:7)" which can only come from fellowship with Jesus Christ.

WELL, IT'S MONDAY

As I look out the cafe window, studying the March clouds, I'm reminded that clouds do look different during the spring season than in the summer storm season, than in the breezy fall season, than in the quiet snow of winter. Mid- March clouds have that look of "we may dump rain on you, or we may not. . . but probably will" look about them. The spring winds, though, always remind me of J explaining to Nicodemus that the wind will blow where it will, not telling us where it came from or where it intends to go, much like the movement of the Holy Spirit in and around our lives (Jhn 3:8). Sometimes we feel the presence of God, oftentimes we don't.

The March wind comes and goes, sometimes violently bending the still unclothed limbs, and we feel it. Maybe the fact that Easter is approaching is what makes me think about God in the wind. It's almost like the warmer weather is being forced on us, or the kingdom of God is coming and must be dealt with. So, how do I tie this in with the theme of today's blog?

Christ has entered the city for one final Passover. Change is coming. The Man who brought a message of love is about to be brutally murdered because some religious leaders couldn't deal with who he really is, the Son of God.

Meanwhile, the air is light and breezy, it feels good on skin covered by coats and jackets all winter long. Spring is about to come again. Dead seeds fallen to the ground will rise from the earth again to feed the hungry. They had to die in order to realize their destiny, their purpose.

It bothers us. We want the love, we want the peace that comes with that love, but not the cost, even if we don't have to pay it. Love has to die. There seems to be no way around it. "Something is coming and you can't stop it," the wind seems to say with greater force each new day as spring approaches.

I need to take a deep breath for a minute. One of the nuances of my blog is to begin with a thought and do a quick reflection on it, which is why I limit myself, generally, to 500 words. I want to get in and out quickly without belaboring or over thinking an idea. And let's face it, there's something cool about having that "eureka!" moment. Look at what I just discovered! Wow! The problem is that for the idea to stick, I need to reflect on that thought and what it can ultimately reveal to me.

God shows me something new, or gets me to look at something a little deeper or in a different light, and I get a sudden caffeine like rush. Happens to me in church all the time, but I've usually forgotten it by the time I get in my car and turn on the ignition. "Man, I've never thought about that before!" Then the radio plays a cool song, and I'm like: "Wait a minute. What was I thinking about?"

That's why I'm revisiting this blog (and the ones to follow), it feels like God wants me to go deeper with this idea. Reflecting on the death and life of Christ is an easy thing, and dare I say it, a pleasant thing on the windy days that follow all the snow, ice, and slumber. But it was just a moment, how often (other than Sunday mornings) have I really reflected on the death and life of my savior? I'm supposed to die everyday after all. Of course, dying everyday takes a conscience effort from the moment I wake up. When I wake up, all I'm thinking about is which coffeehouse house to go to this time.

Right now, I'm going to think about it. There are three things this blog is trying to get me to think about: God is love, love is opposed, and that love had to go away to send us comfort. I don't need, at this moment, to rush off and reread the pertinent chapters (1 Corinthians 13, John 3, and the Passion accounts in the Gospels) again. I need to reflect on them. No, that's not quite right either, they need to sink in on a soul level. God is love and there is an active evil trying to keep me from that love, or at the very least, keep me from feeling that love, or worse yet, get me to believe that it's gone. Maybe that is why the Holy Spirit is called the Comforter by J. Comfort is desperately needed in the midst of a seemingly unending opposition to love. It's not only a war out there, it's a war right here in my heart and it's not ending anytime soon.

"I've felt the presence of that abundant life in what I've called elsewhere moments of 'joy out of nowhere.' A joy that can only come with feeling the presence of the Holy Spirit when I'm not expecting it."

HATE, PART 2

I'm thinking now about the really great, loud thunderstorms that I used to watch and listen to when I was growing up in eastern Kansas. You could literally feel the thunder at the most exciting moments. I missed them this morning and as if God were reminding me he was there, a few distant rumbles managed their way through the walls and windows of my house. I liked it. It's spring, and I want my windy rain storms and the noisy rumblings overhead of angels bowling somewhere up above the clouds. That's what spring weather should be like, it doesn't depress me, these endless cloudy London- like rainy days. I want them. I want summers to be hot and sunny. I want snow in the winter, and I want to find myself swarmed by the red, brown, and yellow leaves of fall as they well, fall all around me. I want things the way they're supposed to be.

We all, however, want to be unique, including me. We want to be rebels, which, of course, will make us unique. But we want things to be "how they're supposed to be" anyway. If we work hard and treat others well then we should reap our rewards. That's how things are supposed to be. We are told, mostly by non- Christians, that the Christian life is easy/breezy. No worries here. God will take care of all our earthly needs and give us the desires of our hearts (like financial well being, a wonderful spouse, and so on) once we choose to follow our Savior.

Yet, there is that real life that we wake up to even on the good days. We feel opposed. We're doing the best we can but Karma doesn't seem to be holding up to its end of the bargain. A walk through J's words in John chapter 15 are sobering even while offering us hope— in the future. "Sudden war is upon us whether we wish it or no."

It doesn't feel right let alone fair. We have to fight for everything non- believers do in life plus deal with the expectations of our Christian walk from both believers and skeptics. And then there is the matter of our own expectations of that walk. It's a war out there and evil will fight us even if we don't fight back. Christianity is a war. One we fight on our knees in prayer and one we fight in the way we handle those things that oppose us and our faith.

OK, What am I trying to accomplish here? This blog is supposed to be about the war we face as Christians as it has and continues to affect my life. Global theology aside, upon closer inspection, my life not only feels but looks like a war. I mean, I definitely feel opposed. What I need right now is focus. My right to abundant life, or some semblance of what I seem to believe that it should look like is being opposed. It may sound a little dramatic to put it in those terms but Christ promised me abundant life and I want it.

I've felt the presence of that abundant life in what I've called elsewhere moments of "joy out of nowhere." A joy that can only come with feeling the presence of the Holy Spirit when I'm not expecting it. Something is actively trying to keep me from that life. I can choose to give up and pretend it's all a dream, but I can't because I have had personal experiences that tells me that kind of life does exist.

Or I can choose to ignore evil but evil will not ignore me. I can pretend it doesn't exist but my experience and the world all around me tells me otherwise. Or I can choose not to fight that evil but it will fight me anyway.

Experience has taught me that as well. I choose to fight.

HEAVEN

For some reason the other day, I thought about a television show I was watching a few years ago while channel surfing. The show featured an interview with actress Natalie Portman. At one point during the interview she pretty much out of the blue stated that she did not believe in a literal heaven and said that it was a crutch for people. I don't remember the context of what caused her to say that, but I thought it sad that she felt that way. Her statement did get me thinking about what I thought about heaven, however.

I believe in a literal heaven, and I expect to be there someday. What surprised me, though, is that while I believe in a literal heaven, I don't think about it that much. It certainly isn't a crutch for me. It's just one of the many facts of my faith that I take for granted. J said he was going to prepare a place for us, yet I haven't thought much about it other than to hope it has Hills Bros French Vanilla coffee which, by the way, is no longer available here on Earth.

My favorite quote from my favorite author, CS Lewis, goes something like this, "aim at heaven and you get Earth thrown in. Aim at Earth and you get neither." I think I'm writing this more for myself than for others. It doesn't matter to me what heaven will look like when I get there. I've been aiming too low. J said the Kingdom of Heaven was near which, in turn means "abundant life" should be as well.

I think I just understood a little of what was said somewhere in the New Testament that "the violent take [the Kingdom of Heaven] by force."

I hope I'm not jumping around too much here. There are moments of joy that come out of nowhere, which sustain me in those more common moments when I feel opposed in life and by circumstances in life. Why can't I just enjoy something/ anything that is not tainted in some way? Abundant life is constantly under assault, and let's face it, if we're honest, it feels like a war a lot of the time. The harder I reach out for joy, the more it feels like something is trying to keep me from it. If there is no heaven then why is it being opposed so strongly? And abundant life, why don't I fight harder for it? Especially when those unexplained moments of joy seem to be telling me, "this should be the norm not the exception."

I've been avoiding this one. It feels too big. How can I expound on subjects like "the Kingdom of Heaven" when the more I read about it and study Christ's descriptions (or analogies, see the parables in the Gospel of Matthew in particular), the more complex I find it to be. The Kingdom of Heaven is at the very least an immense, powerful, fearful, and desirable place that deserves my attention, and maybe even preoccupation.

In this blog, however, the consideration of the very real fact of a heaven I hadn't (haven't) thought enough about, gave way to a more immediate desire of mine, something Christ refers to as abundant life. I admit, I've been avoiding this one, too. It feels too big to tackle in an afternoon at a coffeehouse, perhaps because it is, and also there's this nagging feeling that I can't write about abundant life with any degree of certainty, let alone expertise, if I'm not experiencing it at the moment.

Fortunately for me, I'm reminded this quite unusually rainy July afternoon, that I don't have to figure it out today. Maybe there is nothing to figure out at all. Abundant life isn't a destination, but it is a part of the journey. At the least, it's not a place I can realistically expect to land and never depart from or a country from which I can never be expelled. It isn't a state of mind, either. I can't close my eyes and pretend that I have it or kid myself into believing it will never leave the next time I'm blessed to have the experience.

I don't need to remind myself of this today, especially since I'm feeling a little better about things than I was yesterday. I'm not foolish enough to confuse this current feeling of peace, if not joy, with the attainment of that elusive abundant life. This joy is here today to remind me that there is something that while it feels unattainable, is still worth fighting for everyday.

God does give me, through the Holy Spirit, these moments of unexpected joy that help me through the day to day trials of an often mundane existence. I know how to react to these moments, as gifts to be both grateful and thankful for while they last.

"I know abundant life is out there."

THE CALL OF THE MORNING BIRD

"The call of the morning bird at daybreak lets me know winter has given way to spring. Today, I notice for the first time the arrival of color outside my library window. It may have been there for weeks, it may have sprung from limbs just before dawn. It does not matter. Today, the bird called out to me, "Nature has awakened from its slumber. And so should you."

It finally happened. The Cherry Blossom tree outside my library window began to bud this morning, but not like in the previous six springs. By now, they should already be a brilliant white, looking like a stunning field of lilies captured on tree limbs. A sight I'd begin to mourn the passing of as the leaves gave way to the more familiar summer green.

Unfortunately, this year the death- like sleep that is the winter hibernation season lingered on too long. Most of the buds that have managed to emerge are a dull red mixed in with the precious few strong enough to reach their early April beauty. What is to become of the rest? Will they limp into the green season or just give up all together?

I wrote that about a week ago. The next morning, the day was greeted by the loud buzz of bees swarming the tree. The sound was intense and almost frightening. There was an intentionality that filled the still brisk morning air.

This scene was repeated for a couple of days and then the bees were gone just as fast as they had appeared and the tree had blossomed into its full springtime beauty. The bees had come to the rescue, doing one of the things they were created to do, that is to help nature awaken from its slumber.

I know abundant life is out there if I can just get out of the bed of despair that seems too heavy to lift out of on many days lately. Just before the sun begins to rise, the morning birds call out, singing, "the day is going to begin with or without you." If I can find the resolve, or stubbornness, to rise out of this bed and immerse myself in the Word, even if it's just for a short time, then I can find the strength to face the day and even enjoy the beauty awakening all around me.

Up until recently, it was certainly a battle to get out of bed and face the tediousness of another day just like the many before that promised me little or nothing in return for my efforts. I can't say much has changed in my day to day life from a standpoint of economics and opportunities, but I'm feeling a little better about my day to day life.

What's changed in the last three months? Mindset wise, quite a bit. Writing this blog has had an unexpected consequence, or rather benefit. It has helped my focus. Not just on getting on with my life in the "day to day" experience, although that is a nice part of what is going on here. I'm praying more. I'm thinking more about theology, and as a result, I'm finding now that I'm able to find rest in Christ more than I have in a long time.

It's one thing to write a poem or a blog about taking up J's offer to cast my burdens on him. It's quite another thing to actually do it.

I know for myself, that it's much harder, almost impossible, to rest period when things are not going my way. Especially when nothing seems to be going my way. I'm supposed to go to Christ to receive his rest, but if I'm honest, the reality is that if I'm going to get that rest, he's going to have to bring it to me. And fortunately, He does.

The beauty of theology, for me anyway, is that I not only learn more about my Creator/Lord/ Father/Friend when I am engaged in it, theology is literally the "study of God" after all, but it also brings me closer to him. That's an obvious assessment, I know. The bonus is, or extra credit to keep the analogy going for a moment, that I'm spending more time with him. And that's what our Father desires, communication with his children.

A blog I wrote just a few days ago touches on CS Lewis' idea that we were, in a sense, designed to *run* on God. It's certainly true that I have more energy and passion not just for Christ but for life in general when I am focused on him. Here, I am coming back to that whole abundant life thing again.

I imagine if I were to have any marching orders for myself today it would be to keep moving forward. Christ encourages us to worry about today and let tomorrow worry about itself. Amazing how Christ's words and wisdom all tie together. Christ's calling us to rest in him enables us to let tomorrow be anxious for itself.

"Beauty is a woman waiting to be ravished by an attentive man. But my mind, it wanders."

FOCUS

For whatever reason, that is one of my favorite lines of poetry that I've ever written. I guess I felt it to be particularly clever at the time I wrote it. Today, I'm thinking about it in a different way. It's been a week since I've posted on my blog, and I feel like I should write something. Anything. The trouble is, I'm not feeling all that clever, or insightful for that matter. I'm unfocused and that leads to my biggest enemy, apathy. Today is in danger of being wasted because I don't feel like I have anything important to do or say.

The strong winds of spring feel good as they tug on the hair of my arms, and I just want to drift away with them into Elysium. "Years pass faster than days." I know that on some (most) days, I just have to keep moving. Take a walk. Read the Word. Go to work. Remember to treat others well whether I'm in the mood to or not.

The words of CS Lewis come to mind once again, "everyone we meet we either help send to heaven or help send to hell." OK, there it is, purpose, something important to focus on even though it won't get me a book deal or a pat-on-the-back from the world. This day can and should mean something. I can, if I choose, go to bed tonight with the words "well done good and faithful servant" whispered in my ears as I lay down to sleep.

YEARS PASS FASTER THAN DAYS

Years pass faster than days as the twilight approaches. An oncoming train, a light at the end of the tunnel, or perhaps the descending Morning Star racing toward the end of the age. I know the Christ once felt age slowly tearing at his temporary home as the moon turned the page possibly bringing on an illicit smile from a certain far spent demon's face.

Yet the years they no longer race for a Messiah ascended, and I'm left here to consider a life lived and a life attained by a Lord who lived the life, crossed the threshold, and beckoned us to take up the crisscrossed wood with both wrinkled hands, letting the overused watch fall back into the pocket.

"I'm the good one!"

I'M NOT THE PRODIGAL SON

Every once in awhile, a nuance in a song, a movie, or a book will arise from out of the complacency that comes from the expectations built in from the multiple listenings,

viewings, and readings to stir something inside me. I almost skipped over the parable of the Prodigal Son this morning. I've read it a "million times," so I get it. I understand. I've even been that guy. But it was a long time ago. Since then, I've grown as a man and as a Christian. What struck me this morning was the reaction of the faithful son.

In the Gospel of Luke, he doesn't show up until the end. And he's mad. He's stuck it out. He's been faithful in all things and wonders why the party isn't for him. He's earned it, after all. His father's words, "all I have is yours," don't resonate. "I'm the good one!," he seems to be saying. "I'm the one who has stuck it out and done the right thing. Doesn't that count for anything?"

I'm not the Prodigal Son, I'm that guy. I've done my best to live the Golden Rule, you know, love my neighbor as myself, put others feelings ahead of my own. Another bad thing, maybe a small thing, happens and I'm thinking "not even this can go right (or without a fight) for me?," on many days. I've put the work in, where is the party in recognition of my fighting the good fight? I haven't asked for it, but where is it?

Sometimes, I just have to take a deep breath and remember the Father's words, "all I have is yours," even when I can't feel the comfort those words should bring. The other half of the phrase, "you are always with me," is a reminder of what J has said elsewhere, "I am with you always, to the end of the age."

Thank you, Lord, for a little perspective as I continue to fight through the enemy occupied territory that lies between myself and the prize.

YOUR PRAYER

My Father, you are in heaven; praise is what I owe you. Praise from my flesh praise from my spirit; bring your kingdom down from heaven. Your physical place so far away from here; we want your will to be done down here on earth like it is in your heaven. But it isn't. Give all your children bread daily, raise up the cup of living water to their thirsty lips; forgive my errant thoughts, words, and deeds.

Teach me to forgive and to forget the thoughts, the deeds, and the words of others that molest my peace of mind; Lord, lead me through the ancient, innocent mountain paths far away from the valley of sudden temptation. Free me from the evil intent of mortals and immortals; for Your creation is your kingdom, rebel or servant, evil or hero, for you are the source of all power, you are the source of all glory.

Forever and ever and ever on creation exists by the promise of Messiah, His swoon of death to flight of life; eternity's eyes are lit up by Christ; so be it. Amen. Alleluia. Amen. It is so.

"I need the overwhelming presence of a God that's there waiting for me."

I SEA ETERNITY

I didn't see the ocean until I was thirty years old. I was on tour as the audio guy/ driver for a Southern Gospel group called The Cumberland Boys a few years back, and they knew I had never seen the ocean in person. So, we took a detour while heading south from New York to Georgia for our next concert, so I could get my first experience. The stop was Morehead Beach in North Carolina. We couldn't see the ocean from where we parked, but I could hear it. It was as if I could hear eternity in the distance.

I jumped out of the van and ran across the parking lot and down the beach to the edge of where the water stopped before it receded back into itself. I remember staring out across the water that seemed to vanish into eternity. It was peaceful. There was an immenseness about it that seemed to affirm the presence of a big God. A steady God.

That's what the ocean means to me. The steadiness of God. The peace of God, you know, the kind of peace that surpasses our understanding. I haven't had the opportunity to go and meet God in this context in over two years, and my soul feels the absence. I could try to substitute the experience by going to an isolated lake. If it's a big lake like Lake Michigan it can almost feel like the real thing, but it isn't. I need the real thing.

I see where this is going now. I can listen to Christian music when I'm depressed and it helps, a little, for awhile, sometimes. I can put "The Passion Of The Christ" in my DVD player, and I'll definitely feel it until it's over. Like lakes, these point to the real thing, but they're not the real thing. I need the ocean. I need the overwhelming presence of a God that's there waiting for me. To give me peace.

"If I hear the wind howl, if I hear "hallelujah" in its cry, have I heard an angel sigh or sing the song he was born to live? If I hear a low rumbling in the river while I walk along its shores, if I hear it whisper "I AM still here," have I heard nature speak the truth?

If I hear the ocean's timeless tides, whispering up and down the shoreline, 'future, past, and present, future, past, and present,' will I finally know I'm not alone?"

OASIS OR FRIVOLITY?

"I'll take the enchanted forest tonight, follow the lone doe as she drifts back into the familiar neighborhood of ancient trees, their struggling saplings, and their fallen grandparents. I feel your heartbeat as you follow along through the leaf and limb covered pathway, my friend, a little unsure of why you feel compelled to join me in this quest for *who knows what?*"

I'm remembering how I felt when I was writing the above paragraph. I was feeling hopeful, the journey at that time, if not exciting, was at least fun. Things were going well, and I had ample time to engage with my creativity and create new worlds. The forest beckoned with the promise of hidden worlds and creatures yet to be explored, and more importantly, enjoyed. So, I entered.

Not long after that, the forest turned into a wilderness. Mythical creatures gave way to very real monsters. The wilderness implies adventure, but it also implies imminent danger. Those ominous sounds we hear behind dark tree limbs are being made by things we can't quite see. It's as if the bright, full moon lighting the path and highlighting the trees, also darkens the regions on either side of the path behind the trees.

I'm not feeling under any particular assault today. Or any feelings of frivolity, either. It's a Saturday, and I have a few moments where I have nowhere in particular to be. The sun will fade behind the horizon in a few hours, taking with it much of the oppressive summer heat. Will the evening sky bring with it "fairies dancing with lightning bugs on and around the near autumn- clothed leaves" or "desolate coal chalk arms outstretched against the somber, silver sky?"

Now that I think of it, it may be neither. It will, at least, be a part of the journey. Two weeks from now, I may not even remember it. Kind of nice not worrying for a few hours about having to have a profound moment, which in itself is a an important moment. There's something, dare we say, biblical about being still. About resting, so we can make it to the finish line, scarred as we will be from assaults past and still to come, with knowing smiles on our lips.

THE PARABLE OF FARMER JESUS

If you've been following this blog for awhile, then you know the concept (probably the wrong term) of the Kingdom of Heaven has been on my mind a lot lately. In an earlier blog, "The Kingdom Of Heaven," I was thinking in terms of how it applied to J wanting us to have abundant life here on Earth. Yet, as I've gone back and looked up the various references by Christ, I've become even more convinced that the Kingdom of Heaven, while very important, was not intended to be simple.

Today, I found myself in the parables in the Gospel of Matthew and they all seem to be about the nuances of the Kingdom of Heaven. The one that jumped out at me today in particular was the parable of the weeds. In it, the good sower plants good seed and an enemy follows behind him, sowing in bad seed to contaminate the crop (see Matthew, chapter 13).

It's a familiar parable that's not hard to understand: good people and bad people are living side by side with the bad ones trying to corrupt the good ones. The eventual outcome of the harvest is one of comfort for the good seed and horror for the bad.

OK, so what does this have to do with my understanding something of the Kingdom of Heaven? It comes in J's explanation of the parable to his disciples. The parable compares the kingdom to the sower of the good seed. J explains that it is the Son of Man (ie, himself) who is the sower of the good seed, which he explains are the "sons of the kingdom."

This is the aspect of the Kingdom of Heaven that I'm hearing today.

It plants "good" into the world, which is what J did at the beginning of creation and reaffirmed and reasserted in his life and work here on Earth. I remember a live recording of a song by Resurrection Band called "Jesus Is All." J is, indeed, all in all, so I guess I shouldn't be surprised to find the Kingdom of Heaven within all that he is to us.

One final thought on this parable: J describes us as "sons of the kingdom. (Matt. 13:38)" It's a very subtle reference to our adoption as children of God. We are part of a kingdom that has been invaded by evil and this very short parable gives a quick overview of the war we've been born into and our quite special place within it.

The Kingdom of Heaven is a big universe, and I'm looking forward to continuing to grow in my understanding of it. This is one aspect of the kingdom that I want to spend more time considering. Who knows what tomorrow will bring?

CALLING HUNGRY

A week or so ago, I woke up from a dream where I was writing a song called "Calling Hungry." That's happened to me before, both in dreams and when awake. I'll hear what I think is potentially a great song in my head, and I end up disappointed because I have absolutely no musical talent whatsoever. Fortunately, some friends of mine, who do have that talent have turned a few of my poems into songs, so I guess I can call myself a songwriter. I also had the good fortune to collaborate with a guy, Kevin Reinen, whom I would call a "musical mad genius" to create a progressive rock concept CD, *The Eyes Of Ezekiel,* back in 2009.

"Calling Hungry" the song will likely never get written but the idea won't quite leave me alone. In my dream, I was trying to decide whether it was a romantic song or a song of faith. Now that I've had some time to think about what it was getting at, it kind of feels like a psalm. I feel like I've been running through the kind of dark forest we read about as kids in the old fables and fantasies for some time now and can't seem to find my way of escaping.

Yes, there are those days when the sun breaks through the clouds and brings with it some respite from the trials and tribulations that come with living a life that is opposed, but those days are rare right now.

Calling Hungry. That's what I'm doing when I'm reaching or calling out to J, as I run through or from the wilderness. I know I can't make it to the end of the race on my own. CS Lewis wrote somewhere that God is the fuel we were designed to run on. If we ignore him, then we run the risk of spiritual starvation; and we are spiritual beings after all. I'm calling/ crying out to J precisely because I'm hungry. Spiritually hungry.

Perhaps, I'm at my best when, like Dickens' "Oliver," I hold up my empty hands to God and ask, "sir may I have some more, please?"

THE BASEBALL METAPHOR

The much welcomed rainstorm, though ephemeral, lasted long enough to take the sting off of the heat of the afternoon. The sun, though actually heading in the opposite direction of the rain clouds, has reemerged with a more early spring like feeling in the air. It has brought with it a literal lazy, hazy Sunday afternoon as well and the day's in danger of slipping away.

Meanwhile, I heard a great sermon this morning from Pastor Dave. I really wish I could channel just a portion of the excitement he brings with him everywhere he goes. Why? Because there seems to be a certain amount of energy I need to feel in order to feel like I can accomplish something other than the laundry. It's a voice that says, "work on it tomorrow when you've got more time and desire to get something done."

I'm not a big baseball fan, but I'm familiar with the term "trying to hit one out of the park every time." That's a problem, or desire, I can relate to quite frankly. I have two ideas for blogs that I'm looking forward to writing and exploring from what I heard and learned this morning from Pastor Dave's sermon. But I'm tired, and the clock is ticking, and hitting a feeble ground ball single doesn't feel like it's worth the time bothering with. And, I don't want to go out swinging, either.

The monster called Apathy is throwing knuckle balls at me trying to force me out of the inning. That's fine. The rain delay was refreshing, and I'm leaving soon to have dinner with a friend who is one of my spiritual strength and conditioning coaches. The day is not lost because training (ie, church, fellowship, and the Word) helps me to be stronger when it's imperative that I step up to the plate and deliver for myself or someone else.

The great home run hitters like Babe Ruth and Hank Aaron didn't hit home runs every game or even every week. Even without checking their career stats, I can be sure they played a lot of games and made impacts at different levels in those games when they didn't hit a home run or even get a hit at all. They're remembered by history for the number of homers they hit, but they are in the Hall of Fame because they gave all they had even when there was no glory to be had for hitting singles or making a routine play with their gloves. It's the unnoticed, routine plays that prepared them to make the big plays when called upon.

How does this fit my walk of faith? It's been said elsewhere that character is defined as "doing the right thing when no one is looking." I think there's a lot of truth in that statement. Doing the little, or rather, little noticed things that are a part of our faith, like loving others, striving not to sin, and live a life of commitment makes us strong enough, and prepares us, for when we are called to do the greater things.

Keep swinging and among all the singles, the occasional ball will find its way out of the park. Not when I'm swinging for the fences necessarily but when that home run is needed for someone else even if to my eyes, it merely looks like a blooper into right field.

ANYONE INTERESTED IN TAKING A WALK?

"The moonlight arrives late in the long, hot days of August. There is that often unnoticed world between sundown and starlight called dusk where deer and other night creatures dare to emerge from forest and foxholes to watch the sunset with poets, prophets, and lovers. They come in silence, alone not alone, to the edge of what we call the civilized world: a land of traffic lights and flashing neon signs."

I'm thinking about journeys right now. It's really just one journey we're on, though. We're heading somewhere. The question is will we all end up at the same destination?

Sometimes, I relish in the fact that it seems like it's just J and me on this journey. But that's kind of selfish. OK, not so much selfish as there is nothing wrong with having quality time with someone you love. Still, I didn't start writing this to talk about my quality time with J.

I'm on this journey, with all the love, drama, adventure, and even comedy that comes with it, and I want everyone to join me. I don't have any profound words right at this moment to convince those not on this journey but it's important. We're all on a journey heading toward the end of an adventure. What if we had a chance to end that journey at the same place? That could only mean joy for all, right? I believe in that destination, heaven, even though I don't think much about it because the journey itself demands most of my attention.

Today, it's on my mind again: the journey I'm on and my desire to share that journey with others. Not the day to day struggles and victories, though I think we don't want to go through them alone, but the grander experience. The experience that is not only the feeling that there is something bigger going on here but the knowing that something bigger *is* going on here. I think I will end here, if for no other reason than that the day after day obligations are calling, and also, I don't want to ramble on on this subject. The weekend is upon us, and if nothing else, I have given myself some homework to do.

THE OLD BONE REVIVAL

"You can feel the breeze as it stings blood shot eyes squinting in the desert wind, though the cool air against hair attached to sun burnt skin feels good. You know it is there beyond the haze of floating sand particles agitated at the arrogance of the wind disturbing their rest. The cold of moonlit, cloudless nights brought sleep like death for days on end to the bones of those who accepted its offer. But the Wind!, who like prophecy, fills the land with an expectancy of Pentecost, does not care. Dust, wet with the changing air, marries dust, and you can feel it."

I'm thinking, today, about how many of the Psalms were lamentations of pain, frustration, and despair. It's OK to show that side of ourselves to God. Someone once noted that the Psalms always have a happy ending.* The interpretation here is that no matter what: everything's OK! But a day or moment in my life is not a song or psalm with a set beginning or end. The story continues on.

Yes, there is a happy conclusion to this journey if we stay the course but days don't always end on a happy note nor do many of our experiences. Dry bones will be revived, metaphorically speaking, when we meet our Savior in the sky (read about it in the epistles of St. Paul). To use another image, this wilderness I'm walking through does not promise a happy end to my life on Earth or even an occasional happy trail. It merely promises to block or hinder my journey any way it can.

*Incorrectly, I found out later.

There are days, let's admit it, that we'll go to sleep without the happy conclusion having arrived or even the happy moment, the joy out of nowhere. This is one of those days for me. Sometimes the bones feel so dry and brittle it takes all my strength to keep moving toward the revival of body, mind, and soul I've been promised but can't yet see. Some days, the wind just doesn't seem to be blowing. At least I can't feel it for any number of reasons.

This is not the end to a happy day, nor an ending at all, it's another day in the battle for our lives. I do feel strong enough to admit it and accept that it's part of the war we find ourselves in. Tomorrow, I may wake to the caressing of a refreshing wind, or I may not, but the journey continues. No matter how weary I get or how cold the dark of the wilderness becomes, I will continue to walk the path I am on. Even if it feels more like a stubborn determination than a rally cry.

THE WIND IS COMING

"The wind is You, every shade of cool and hot. The wind is You, every brush of breeze or gust, and I, sitting here (sort of sweating but not quite) breathing in, breathing out nothing other than You."

We're in that time of year (September) when summer is drifting ever so slowly away into the past and the fall, an impending storm of wind and change from frivolity into slumber, has yet to show its face. I'm reminded of this by the pile of dead, brown leaves strewn out along a street I drove past this morning. Fall is approaching but we won't see it until the signs are already there.

One day soon, I'll awake to the trees already seemingly days into their transformation, and I'll have read the "signs of the times" in the leaves and refreshingly cool gusts of winds after the fact. Experience has taught me that despite my diligence and desire, fall will begin its transformation without me, and I'll be a little disappointed in myself.

So, I take a moment and think, "what else will I miss?," or "what else *have* I missed?" The presence of the Holy Spirit, the giver of peace, can't be seen but can be felt or maybe more accurately, noticed. I want it in a larger way than I even want to see the beginning of fall. Yet, watching for it doesn't improve my chances. What I'm getting at here is what CS Lewis calls the "surprise of joy" and what I call the "joy out of nowhere," that surprising moment when the presence of the Spirit, which was already there, comes to my attention. Like the fall in full force, there's that moment when the Wind blows and my whole mind and spirit has a freshness blown into it.

This is not a teaching moment. I can't teach myself, let alone others, how to anticipate this gift. I'm always surprised by it and it rarely lasts for long but it reminds me that I'm not alone. I guess it's the first few hints of fall that has me thinking and anticipating that which I can't capture. The Spirit is as untamed as the wolf roaming the outskirts of town, and there's no point in trying to capture it. What I can do is pray, reflect, and read the Word, and I can rest in knowing that once again, the wind will come and refresh me whether I happen to see it coming or not.

THE LORD IS OUT THERE SOMEWHERE

A wolf howls loudly through the silent, mid- winter night while pangs of loneliness stir my soul to join him in his cries up to the foreboding sky. The Lord is out there somewhere in the dark of night, I know because I can feel the Spirit stir through leafless trees and matchless stars.

The Holy Ghost whispers and walks through the sleeping forest outside, a place my soul both longs and fears to go, beckoning it to come and reside and fight in the land where battle fronts call out for the hero in our hearts. Stir, I say to my blood run cold, the wolf won't wait forever.

The Lord leads him on through the night, through barren hill tops and forest paths on to something more, the cause, the fight, the reason to hold its head up high again. The Lord, he resides somewhere in the night. Spirit, draw the cover from my soul turn it from fear to joy in promise leading from pit to wellspring to whole.

"Purpose. That's a word that has haunted me my entire adult life."

OF BOREDOM AND NIGHTMARES

Sometimes, rereading things I've already written, whether it's an essay, a blog, a lyric, a book, or a poem reminds me of something I haven't thought about in awhile. It helps me to remember what I felt, especially on days like this when I'm not feeling anything in particular. So, here it goes, time to pull out an old book, turn to a random page, and see what comes of it.

"In my dreams continual, point unsung, I walked nameless streets lined with gray. In my dreams continual, never ending, streets lined with gray. For days on end, on end, the nameless streets. For days on end, the nameless streets. I walked the streets lined gray. Ever? No, never an end. Just the gray."

I remember vividly what I was going for: trying to creatively describe the frustration of a journey that did not appear to have a destination. It helps to know, or at least feel like, you know where you're heading. Purpose. That's a word that has haunted me my entire adult life. Making money isn't enough. Being the "nice guy" isn't enough. I want to feel like I'm making a real difference in people's lives, whether it's through my writings or my interactions with people on a daily basis. When I feel like that isn't happening, well, the paragraph above is a pretty accurate description of how I'm feeling and no well meaning platitude or Bible verse emailed by a friend or family member is going to help.

The excerpt is early on in a chapter from my fantasy novella titled "I Awoke From A Dream," but probably should be called "I Awoke From A Nightmare." In this early chapter of *The Journey Into Know*, the protagonist is suddenly released from his prison by the wind, which allegorically speaking represents the Holy Spirit. When the wind blows, good things happen to him and the created world in general. I need the Wind to blow through me and "blow out" the things that cover my life like a dense fog, impairing my ability to see my journey clearly now as much as ever.

"Something like the wind pulled the veil covering my eyes and in that instant I watched the silky, gray cover vanish delicately from my sight. In two steps I stopped, stunned. I had been walking. For how long, only creation knew. For me, it was all a nightmare waking. This new reality felt more real than the time I had lost, spent in oblivion."

The Wind will lead the man on a journey of personal discovery and purpose. Amen, let it be so.

LEGACY

Funny how some bands or writers have a knack for saying something you're thinking about or needing to hear. Stryper is a band that often fills that role for me. I just heard one of their new songs "Legacy" online. I wonder what mine would be if J took me home today?

Legacy is one of those tricky words. Wanting to leave a legacy means wanting to leave a lasting impression on others. But doesn't that mean wanting to feel more important than the next guy? It reminds me of a question I like to think I made up but probably heard somewhere, "can a humble person know that he or she is humble?"

Much like the old joke, "everyone serves as an example, even if it's just a bad one," we all leave our own legacies. "Nice guys finish last," but they are remembered with fondness and serve as examples to those who were affected by their kindness and compassion. They are the often nameless standard bearers we try to emulate in our own lives and pass on to others. Where I'm heading with this is back to J's command to "love others as we love ourselves.(Matt.19:19) " J always put (and puts) our needs before his. That's one of the reasons the world remembers him even if just merely as a great man, though he was and is a great deal more than that and that is more important than the fawning skeptics realize.

Speaking of writers, CS Lewis is one who often whispers in my ear. I'm reminded of what he wrote near the end of his exceptional essay, "The Weight Of Glory," "everyone we meet we help send to heaven or help send to hell." I know which side of this story I want to be on. No matter what life throws at me, and that's been quite a bit these past seven years, I'm grateful that despite how I'm feeling moment to moment, day to day, the Holy Spirit still spurs in me the desire to love others like I love myself.

A PSALM OF MAY

Let the red, let the yellow, blue, and green streams of hope promise lavender sunsets. I will walk along the river's muddy shores hearing low whispers, "peace, peace, peace." I will walk below jet gray skyscrapers that prick the passing elephant pastel clouds.

The word on the streets rushes, hushes, rips, lifts, chills, thrills, bends, rends, sends the eyes upward! Back then forth. Streets then alleys then, gone. Fear, no euphoria. Half- known, unknown. The rush. The wonder. The whoosh of mid- May winds. Hints of re- birthing showers.

Word, inhaled that past moment, thrusts back through vocal chords exhales, joy. Timeless moment. Alone, not alone. Walking along with the thousand voice choir singing, pleading with unconscious thoughts.

The rocks cried out, "peace like blue between clouds." Love bent beautiful as yellow sunflower petals, blue- green flowing blades spread across great plains toward that unpicked cherry which descends to ascend. To that end, I walk. Not to the sunset but the sunrise. Each song passed in, passed out.

"Forget the forest for the trees, I want to see more
than just the few feet in front of me."

THE FOG, THE BREAKTHROUGH, AND THE DEEPER MAGIC

These days, I barely have the time to think, pray, dream, relax, or anything else that makes my life feel meaningful. It's times like these when life seems so repetitious and each new day looks like the previous one and tomorrow looks like today, looking like yesterday that a fog seems to envelop me. Forget the forest for the trees, I want to see more than just the few feet in front of me. I've gone through times like these, well not like *these*, before and J has always freed me in what sometimes seemed like a miraculous moment. Of course, the above statement isn't totally true, I know it's a matter of me finding time in the middle of all the mental and spiritual oppression to seek out J, or more rather, see where he is in the midst of this fog I find myself in. Because he is there.

Yes, there is a formula, so to speak, prayer, time in the Word, fellowship, and somehow remembering to "rejoice in the day the Lord has made," even or especially when I don't feel like I am able to. But it isn't magic. It isn't just Satan that likes worn out, ineffective Christians. The world does, too. However, there is a weapon I've found, possibly part of what CS Lewis meant by the "deeper magic" in his series of books *The Chronicles Of Narnia* that has been given to me. J broke life down into two simple commands, "love the Lord your God, and your neighbor as yourself (Matt 19:19)."

J's command, when I apply it in my life, gives me less time to wallow in my own frustrations and grief. It's a hard weapon to pick up and wield when I can't see very far in front of me, but when I fight back, I ultimately feel better about myself. And that is sufficient for the day.

"Past Labor Day into Oktoberfest, past All Hallow's Eve into All Saint's Day, the frivolity of harvest gives way to the coming hibernation of Mother Earth. It's the time of year of my late year New Year's resolution, that is, to put on the brakes long enough to watch the annual parade of colors processional, the fanfare celebrating a time of Jubilee about to come to a land worn from growing, feeding, and sustaining the lives of its inhabitants.

"The Spirit walks along the park, too, singing a quiet lullaby, 'rest now my little ones and close your eyes. I will guard you while you sleep. Though you die now for a time, I'll wake you in the spring with the tears that I weep'."

NATURE'S JUBILEE

Fall is sneaking up on me again. There is a certain joy in watching the changing of the colors of nature, a changing of the guard, if you will. It slows down the pace of my day for a few moments, and I'm able to forget that life is passing by much too fast for me. But usually, I miss it and I feel the disappointment of losing out on the opportunity to enjoy the experience, the slowing down of the rush and crush of life.

Meanwhile, nature dies again so it can be reborn in the spring. It becomes quiet, even if its inhabitants don't follow suit. And I think maybe that's why I hate missing it happen. I desperately need that rest, so I can return again to the fray renewed and ready to resume the fight. I know the moment will come when the quiet born of a snow cloaked neighborhood below the expanse of the clear, evening sky will share with me a momentary joy. That is, until the reality of the bitter cold drives me inside to the safe haven of comforters and fireplaces.

A look back in the Old Testament reminds me that God ordered ancient Israel to celebrate a year of Jubilee every 50 years where, among other things, the land was to be given a year of rest and slaves were to be set free. It could be said that God gives nature a few months of Jubilee every winter so that it can come back strong in the spring to do what it was created to do. It's also why he commanded the Israelites to reserve a day of complete rest for themselves each week.

I'm looking outside now at the trees that have not yet begun to lose this year's clothing, though the fading has begun to occur already, waiting for the chance to share in its Jubilee before the air becomes too cold, and I lose the chance to embrace the moment. If I am vigilant, I will remain atop the watchtower, ready and waiting to share with nature the joy of lying down for a much needed rest.

ACCOMPLISH. . . WHAT?

The old farmer smiled and then laughed loudly, throwing his hands up in the air almost as if he were praising something.

"Of course, of course." He laughed again. "To think, to search, to know!" Again, I involuntarily stepped back.

"Know what?," I asked. I was afraid now. I got the feeling that something was going to be asked of me. Something I might not be able to accomplish.

The protagonist in *The Journey Into Know*, has recently been released from a nightmare and is "out for a walk" on the countryside enjoying the day, for the first time in a long while, just for itself. His encounter with the old farmer and the journey he's about to embark on fills him with fear. And maybe just a little bit of annoyance. Times of refreshment in the Spirit are rare and don't last very long, so we want them to last as long as possible.

But back to the first part, I know, as a child of God, I have something to accomplish. Some days, I'm sure of what that is, other days, I wonder (and worry) if I don't. Still more, if I don't miss out on the opportunity, will I be strong or wise enough to do what I've been called to do by the One (J) who took great care to not only save me but give me a task or purpose? That "journey to know" is a journey that at times scares me and at other times thrills and honors me.

I've had some rough years lately, having my job taken away from me and losing my house and life savings just to name a few things. Since then, I've come to live by this maxim, "I've got to walk the path I'm on." I've referred to that path as one through the thick of an imposing wilderness a lot lately. It feels the same on most days, though the nuances and challenges and fears keep it interesting, for lack of a better way of putting it. I do know that somewhere down this path, I will know what this journey is supposed to teach me, and that "purpose" I struggle to find will be along that path as well. So, I continue to walk at the least knowing that something bigger than me is waiting for me to reach that destination or moment. In those rare moments of clarity, I remember that this will all make sense at the end of the journey.

I'M STILL HERE

"I need a personal God, actually, I need God to be more personal, well, no actually, I need God to feel more personal than he has lately."

I just bought a Tee shirt from a line of shirts that feature crosses in various forms mixed creatively with other images. You wouldn't necessarily know they were Christian themed shirts if not for the one word written sideways on them. The word on this particular shirt is "redemption." One word, the right word, can carry a lot of power. Especially if that word is on your mind or if J wants it to be on your mind.

I haven't thought much about redemption lately. I get the word. J's blood spilled on the cross redeemed and continues to redeem us. I get that, and I'm grateful for it. I would much rather be mentioned in the Book of Life than be in a hand basket, wondering where I'm heading. But that's not what I'm hearing today. Whether I realized it or not, I've been looking for redemption. Surely my run of luck, or lack thereof, is due to bad karma or more accurately sin in my life. OK, I'll just say it, I've had a hard time not feeling like I'm being punished. I have been looking for redemption, and an end to my run of trials or at least a break from them, or even a hint that the light at the end of the tunnel isn't an oncoming train.

Today is a freezing, rainy late winter day in early March. The birds of summer are still on vacation and contemplation appears more relevant than revelation. No pat answers this late afternoon just something to think about. Redemption. I need to feel it more than explain it. Maybe the second most important word right now is "focus."

Focus on redemption rather than wondering why I need to feel redeemed, which isn't accurate anyway in the very possible sense that what I'm really looking for is to be justified as much as feeling the punishment will end, and my being restored, whatever that means.

Now, I'm feeling a little selfish. I've been wallowing in self pity and that really gets one nowhere. What does the word "redemption" look like right now and what is it that J is trying to tell me? The Christian life is not only a journey but a war. Self pity is a sort of self emasculation that doesn't do me any good. "It doesn't matter how hard you can hit. What matters is how hard you can get hit and still keep moving forward. (paraphrase from the film *Rocky Balboa*)." Pressing forward when there isn't a clear reason to do so at all is what I need to do everyday. That can be a victory in and of itself. A reason to keep pushing forward.

WONDER

High and higher, that is what you are to me, Lord, God, and Savior. Not aloof but a lifeline. The sun shines, the warm winds blow and joy sits beside me for awhile.

Let go. Large words like analyzation destroy the moment. The lion roaring waits in anger to devour the moment. Peace comes in like a flood but behind it waits sharpened fangs and claws. So much hate stalks the world we live in. Joy brings rest but hate does not rest for fear it will be forgotten. Perhaps that's what the dragon fears most from Man and God, the words "depart from me, I never knew you."

Now, I think I know why praise of the one who started it all releases Joy and her sisters Faith, Hope, and Grace from their silent prisons. Adventure. "Run, don't walk. Climb, don't lie down," I feel my spirit cry out to flesh and bones silently wanting more than TV and late night snacks can offer. Live. Live in the moment, the oasis inside the swirling battles between joy and the dragon. No wonder it, no wait, wonder at it all. Wonder at the honor and attention each soul deserves.

And wonder at the joy and fury the words "holy, holy, holy, Lord God Almighty" command from both the willing and unwilling.

"I want to be blessed, but I don't want to change anything in my own life."

YOU CAN'T HAVE IT BOTH WAYS

Rereading a book that contains so much wit and wisdom like GK Chesterton's *Orthodoxy* is a return to the feet of a great teacher. In it, he talks about the contradictory remarks skeptics use to try to discredit Christianity. One example noted is that Christianity produces weak people fixated on a fantasy land and that it also is a fierce religion that is responsible for all the world's major wars. For more, see the chapter titled, "The Paradoxes Of Christianity."

Basically, those opposed to Christianity, who are generally in favor of their view of J, are trying to have it both ways, in order that we see that Christianity is wrong and/or false in all ways at all times. Of course, that's not true in any way at any time. J's life and death gives us purpose in all things and and at all times and behind that purpose is a will and intent.

As I'm prone to digress, or rather, deviate into another thought, I'm thinking now about having it both ways in my life. I want to be blessed, but I don't want to change anything in my own life. Not that God's blessings are directly linked to our good deeds because obviously they're not, but I want them to be. If I "overcome evil with good," as Paul the Apostle writes in his epistle to the Romans (12:21), then surely I deserve a reward, or at least a spiritual pat-on-the-back, so to speak, whatever that looks/feels like. I do tend to get caught up in the works producing rewards mindset, especially when I feel like life is getting the best of me.

Of course, it's not about my having it both ways, deserving or receiving rewards, overcoming evil, or even receiving an unexpected blessing. It's about the hardest thing of all, for me anyway, it's about waking up in the morning and thanking J for the day and feeling grateful for it even or especially because I don't feel grateful for it. I imagine J says to me on those days what Robin said to Batman in my favorite Batman reboot *Batman Forever.* "You have a real gratitude problem." And if I'm honest, I have to respond, "you are right, sir."

I'm going to allow myself one last digression or deviation in an attempt to sort this all out. How can I have it both ways in my life? I can choose to continue my fight to overcome the evil that surrounds me, and I can thumb my nose at life/evil/Satan when I'm getting beat up and respond "sorry, dude, I'm going to keep saying I'm grateful until I feel it." Living to fight another day isn't about surviving but winning a battle I thought I had lost. I'm here, aren't I? I've survived to write about the experience, and I'm grateful for that.

SUFFICIENT

For a child's innocence, my soul cries out on heavy days. What I would give to dine on milk when a lack of peace stays the food of grace from my mouth. Today, I read about perfection formed by forty days of flood and famine for the man who does not stray from the course determined by God.

The night always ends with the rising of a new day, and I find again the patient one waiting, smiling, and saying once more, "isn't this the day I made?"

"Do I guard my heart? No, I rarely, if ever even think about my heart."

HAVE A HEART

I was reminded of an Old Testament verse recently, "Keep your heart with all vigilance, for from it flows the springs of life (Prov. 4:23)." I don't spend a lot of time in the book of Proverbs for reasons I haven't really considered. Maybe it's the wave after wave of words of advice that can be quite overwhelming. And come to think of it, there aren't any verses that have, up until now, stuck with me.

But recently, I met a nice girl who went to the trouble to have the verse tattooed on her arm. Now that's a long term commitment. So, I thought I would take another look at the verse, and taken by itself, it is actually quite profound.

Do I guard my heart? No, I rarely, if ever, even think about my heart. It's so much easier, at least for me, to think about the hearts of those around me. Maybe it's because I tend to be compassionate by nature (here, I pat myself on the metaphorical back) and try to be a positive influence on other people's lives.

I like to be that guy, the one people can count on. Of course, the bonus of living out the Golden Rule is that it makes me feel good and relevant. That's all well and good, but if I let my heart die aren't I committing a sort of spiritual suicide?

The first thing I have to remember is that it is OK to "guard my heart" as long as I don't get caught up in a victimization mindset. How do I defend my heart without dwelling on the assaults on it? The second part of the verse intrigues me, "because it is the wellspring of life."

First, I must guard my heart against its enemies, but second, it's the source of my ability to defend it. J told the people that he came not to just give us life, but abundant life. It appears that the writer of Proverbs is here foreshadowing the source behind "the wellspring of life," the originator and the power, and importantly, the renewing energy behind it. That's an encouraging thought but not the end, I think.

We are told to guard our hearts. That's the command. We have the responsibility of guarding the heart given to us by God. The war, as we all know, is coming at us whether we want it to or not. So, as what typically happens, J starts with one thought to get me to another. It's not about a victimization mindset, causing me to fight to survive but a victory mindset that there is a power already inside me, which was given to me by J that can resist, and even defeat evil, and that is a comfort. J calls the one he sent the Comforter, after all.

I must guard my heart because it's the wellspring and source of abundant life. My life. It's a positive command for a more practical and purposeful way to approach the trials I face. And I can get behind that mindset.

IS IT HIP TO BE THE TEACHER'S PET?

I recently saw a photo on a friend's Facebook page that was a notebook page with the words "When you are going through something hard and wonder where God is, remember that the teacher is always quiet during the test" written on it, and left the comment "and gives the answers if you show up for class and ask."

It's a quaint phrase designed to bring comfort. Yet, it can be considered a truism of sorts. My first reaction was to remember teachers who would sometimes give pop quizzes when most students failed to show up for class on days when the snowfall in eastern Kansas made it hard to get there.

These teachers would write the answers to the quiz on the chalkboard, thus rewarding the brave minority with a few extra points. I don't think they ever changed the overall outcome of my grades but it was kind of fun to be a part of an inside joke.

Now, I'm thinking about how this applies to the idea of a Teacher who gives answers to those students who make the effort to show up when the weather called life's challenges seem intent on keeping them inside for fear of the discomfort of braving them. Another quaint truism we have all heard is that, "the answers are in the Book (Bible)." True, but we're still here experiencing the inclement weather, wondering where the shelter (comfort) and the food (answers) are to be found.

As long as I'm throwing out truisms, "seek the truth and you will find it" fits the bill. God is a patient teacher, waiting for that rare student who will make a visit to his office to learn the answers to the questions, whatever they may be at any given moment during their lives.

I went to a school, Kansas University, where many classes had 50 or more students in them. I can tell you the teacher feels just as distant from the student as the student does from the teacher. Be one out of the 50 that makes the effort to get one on one teaching from the teacher and they will go out of their way to help you. Not just that day but for the rest of the semester. They're just like us, they need to know that they're being heard, that what they are doing means something.

I think this may be a fair, if flawed, example of how God feels. He desperately wants to be relevant in our lives and responds in kind to those who reach out to him. Yeah, it can be disconcertingly quiet when we are going through tests but having the desire, and let's say stubbornness, to brave the storms to take the quiz, and get the answers, begins to build a stronger long term relationship with our Teacher.

A DISTANT KIND OF TOMORROW (WORTH WAITING FOR)

"The horizon fading below the Atlantic's gray waves appears to tell of only stories past because the sun glides over and away toward the west, leaving the promise and prophecy of tomorrow to a distant land."

Tomorrow, not the day but the promise of a new beginning, seems lost somewhere between the wilderness we walk through and the sun shedding its light on the other side. Tomorrow, the day we stress over today, will arrive with the insistent demand of the alarm clock. "Tomorrow" is the promise of better things to come, the destination we dream and sing about where happy endings and reunions really happen. Tomorrow is New Jerusalem descending, a city we will enter to be reunited with loved ones and protected by the presence of the Lord. We certainly need to feel a hint of that to help us to continue through the ominous wilderness called life.

The breeze blows and for an instant, we feel the peace of the inexplicable, the presence of the Holy Spirit, who touches us to remind us that "tomorrow" with all its peace, rest, and glory is not only coming, it's coming toward us, indeed it is coming for us.

It's early springtime and the winds that blow harder everyday as the celebration of Easter approaches, remind me that the promise of tomorrow is in some sense already here.

"I felt like I was beginning to understand something."

STREAMS OF LIVING WATER

A couple of months ago, I wrote a blog on my thoughts about a verse from Proverbs titled "Have A Heart." The verse reads, "Above all else, guard your heart, for it is the wellspring of life." I've been thinking about that blog and this verse a lot lately, because I've had a nagging feeling that I didn't go far enough in my analysis. The safety of our hearts is kind of a big deal. I alluded to J's assertion that he wants us to have more than just life, he wants us to have abundant life, which if you have been read many of my blogs, you know I'm a bit obsessed with finding that promised quality of life. Maybe that's why I felt like there was more in there than I had previously considered.

A few days ago, I began rereading John Eldredge's *Waking The Dead*. He mentions Proverbs 4:23 early on and also quotes a verse from the Gospel of John, "Whoever believes in me [Jesus] as the Scripture has said, streams of living water will flow from within him (Jhn 3:8)." When I read these two verses side by side it was like a key (John's verse) opening a lock (the verse in Proverbs), and I felt like I was beginning to understand something. The paradox I found in Proverbs in that while we had to guard our hearts because it was the wellspring of life, we, at the same time, needed that wellspring to have the ability to guard it had been perplexing me. Was this some sort of "what came first, the chicken or the egg" irony? What I realized after considering these two verses side by side is that, once again, a verse in the New Testament confirms or explains something from the Old Testament.

Jesus says streams of living water flow from within believers. Proverbs states that the heart is the wellspring of life. Notice the water connection here? This is where I see the connection, if we believe we literally have Jesus in our hearts, and from that wellspring of faith comes the "streams of living water that flow from within." Our faith in Jesus is the "wellspring of life" that gives us the strength to guard our hearts. See the correlation?

Before I leave this subject, I think it's worth noting that there is something awesome going on here. It's not just that faith in Jesus gives us the power to guard our own hearts, we now also have streams of living water that will flow from within us. If that water is flowing from within us, then it is flowing out of us as well, and extends the love and power of our faith in Jesus that can affect the hearts of others. To quote one of my favorite phrases, "pretty cool, huh?"

INTRODUCING, MR. LUKE WARM

I like to read through the Bible in different ways. Sometimes, I'll read my favorite passages (Psalm 23, Isaiah 52:13- 53, John 1:1-14, Philippians 4:4-8 to name a few). Other times, I'll read the four gospels, other times the Gospel of Luke followed by the Acts Of The Apostles. Lately, I've been working through the New Testament only reading the words of Christ. I finished today with his words in the book of Revelation. In chapter three, he chides the church in Laodicea for being too comfortable. A warning follows, "I will spit you out" for being neither hot nor cold (Rev. 3:16).

I hate rereading this passage because it hits me where I live. I'm haunted by a sense of waste. Am I really "about the Lord's business?" Consistently? No, not really. This verse speaks to larger issues like letting the cares of the world chip away at my resolve until the Apathy monster rears its ugly head. Another 70 hour week blows by, or blows me away, and I'm too worn out to fight to find personal time with J let alone find the time to read the Word, let alone study the Word.

At the end of a long and frustrating day or week, I can't find the desire, let alone the resolve to resist the Apathy monster, so I let him win for the night or the week or the month. And I know it's just a cop out on my part. I can ignore evil but evil will not ignore me. Every time I give up an hour or an evening or a day to Apathy, it's more of him and less of me in my life. It becomes harder to answer the call to "wake up, O sleeper" to do whatever it is I'm called to do. Jonah was literally spit out of the whale for running away from what God had called him to do. I don't want to be spit out.

The problem, I've found, is that the Apathy monster gets heavier the longer I let him feed on me. He becomes harder to resist, let alone defeat. It's like trying to lift a heavy box and thrust it onto the top shelf far above my head. And yet, I have to do just that. The good news is that I've done it before, and I can do it again, even though there is a voice whispering somewhere nearby, "that was when you were younger. That was when you were stronger. Just look at you now."

There is a weapon that I've used before, it's called Stubbornness. That part of me that refuses to get played, as it were, by someone or something else. That's the "hot" part of me that can be an asset rather than a hindrance as I try to regain that sense of purpose and urgency that I need to be "about the business," whether I feel up to it or not.

THE CIRCLES OF LOVE
AND TOLERANCE

I heard a sermon about the "circles of love" this morning. The Pastor talked about small circles, including family and friends, and larger circles that included our city, then our state, then our country and so on. It sounds good, loving others and expanding that ability for us to love a wider and wider circle of people. Showing our love to others is a worthy goal or endeavor.

He really didn't go on to explain how that love worked in our lives and expanded into other people's lives other than in the interest of tolerance. Now, tolerance is a good thing, actually it's a great thing. Yet, I found myself thinking "is tolerance the beginning of our ability to love or an end to the means?" Or neither? Certainly, learning to be tolerant will make it easier to feel love for others we might not necessarily love, or tolerate, otherwise. Yet, there must be more to love than merely tolerating others.

I can't consider tolerance without its opposite, intolerance. This morning's sermon didn't mention intolerance but if love shows itself only through tolerance then it seems to be more of a barrier to bad thoughts and actions than an active voice that desires to love no matter whether the loved person appears unlovable at first.

Love is an easy word to throw around because, after all, "love conquers all." Would that it did! The good news is that actually, it does. But to do that, it must really be a love that conquers *all*. It can't be a feeling of good will or tolerance, or even desire, though desire comes closest of all.

Love has to be active, it has to be a verb as well as a noun. Here is why I believe the concept of Christian love, the concept of loving others as ourselves, is the strongest, and most accurate, conception of a love that can make a difference in our circles both small and great.

Loving others as ourselves is the act of putting them on an equal footing with ourselves. It transcends mere tolerance because it envelopes the loved person with that love we all want for ourselves. It's a strong kind of love that isn't only fighting off its inverse, its seeking to be an active participant in the life of those who invoke its name.

To try to sum this all up, a proactive love, one that actively causes us to embrace ourselves and others is much stronger than a passive love whose strength lies in merely showing goodwill by tolerating others. It's still love but it's not a love that can overcome our emotional and spiritual weaknesses. It takes an active good to defeat an active evil. That is why one of the names of God is literally Love.

AN APPEAL TO DESIRE

Before time began, or rather before what we call time, a vast black void filled space, a place called Chaos by makers of myth, desire drove God to speak light into dark.

All that we know, night & day, water & land, beast of ground & air, man & woman, life & death, good & evil co- exist. Some should and some should not. Night & day, partners keeping time, help those few who notice such things, take note of its passing, or rather its moving forward.

Man & woman, ah yes, man & woman desire many things. Often each other. On occasions poets call poetic, one particular man desires a particular woman who, by fate or chance, or whatever it may be called, happens to feel desire for that one particular man who desires her, and that is the circle called love.

God became man to reconcile himself to Man. If that claim is the highest crest of love (and it is) then the Passion Play needs no other name. If an artist desires to take on the guise of his art to walk among his art, will he not laugh & cry (as it does), will he not fix & teach, lead & preach?, will he not then desire that the love he gives be returned?

If we follow the Lord because desire compels us to, out of love, then we will, feeling somehow that to laugh & love is real, real in a sense that chance existence is not, in a sense magnified by the surprise of joy.

The Lord our God, who made the rules, who put the color on the dark canvass, who appealed to our better nature on the cross, then later, in the resurrection, for our reconciliation, leaves us with one unopposable conclusion: that He is a God of desire.

"The moonlight arrives late in the long, hot days of August. There is that often unnoticed world between sundown and starlight called dusk where deer and other night creatures dare to emerge from forest and foxholes to watch the sunset with poets, prophets, and lovers.

They come in silence, alone not alone, to the edge of what we call the civilized world, a land of traffic lights and flashing neon signs. This is the land of Middle Earth for those creatures both human and four legged who come together on country roads and backyards to let the enchantment of not quite day not quite night hold them as the intensity of daytime activity gives way to moonlight and haunted forests."

BIGGER THAN THE LION

Darkness takes over the night sky late at the height of summer in eastern Kansas, which allows the observant time after the work day to watch the sunset from one's porch. The sky over the landscape is much bigger than in the city and storm clouds, no matter how hard they try, can't just sneak up on you. For those who can read the signs in the sky, the incoming clouds from the west, mixing white and gray with a sky transitioning from blue to orange, red to purple to navy blue to finally black provides a chance to set the problems of life aside for awhile to watch a living motion picture.

There is a sort of haunting feeling that comes with stopping long enough to observe the grand beauty of a nature that's big enough to ignore the world around and below it.

A wolf howls in the unseen distance and the world becomes bigger, at first a little frightful, but then more mysterious and eternal. I've missed this, as much as I love the big city with all the hustle and bustle that goes with it, there is definitely a peace that transcends the cares of the world if only until it's time to go to bed.

One of the themes reoccurring in my life lately is the pursuit of abundant life. Can it really be pursued? At least successfully? I'm beginning to think not, it looks more and more like abundant life can be obtained about as successfully by force of will as the "joy out of nowhere" I also want to experience more often. As I sit here, at least, abundant life appears to proceed out of the choices that I make, like choosing to spend time in the Word and choosing to sit outside and watch the storm front roll in.

The storm, may in fact, produce damaging winds and even a tornado but that possibility is exciting even though it may bring danger along with it. Maybe it's exciting because it is dangerous. All this is to say that slowing myself down at times allows me to actually live a little in the midst of all this merely existing. The evil that hunts us on a daily basis wants us to feel hunted moment to moment so we get caught up in the feeling of being able to do little more than escape a danger that won't let us rest. In that sense, the stalking lion has already won. If all we do is concentrate on survival then the thought of actually living doesn't occur to us. At least not to me.

Let the lion roar again tonight. He frightens me at first, but his cries remind me that there's more out there in the wild, something bigger, more mysterious, and eternal that will outlive his power. That is why the night, though it keeps me from seeing much of what is around me, things that will not last, it also excites and comforts me because it allows me to see instead the things that will.

This is all, of course, a metaphor. Yes, the lion (Satan) momentarily has the power to try to steal, kill, and destroy not only my abundant life but also my life itself if I succumb to that fear. And his is a very real threat because evil is relentless like war. But the picture is so much bigger. It may not seem like it when I'm running for my life or standing up in, but losing, the battle. The truth is that the journey I am on will last long after the lion has been defeated. My savior, J, died on the cross, but he rose again and sin and death died with it. That's the big picture. That is why the dark of night, which can momentarily scare me, really inspires me.

"I'll take the enchanted forest tonight, follow the lone doe as she drifts back into the familiar neighborhood of ancient trees, their struggling saplings, and their fallen grandparents. I feel your heartbeat as you follow along through the leaf and limb covered pathway, my friend, a little unsure of why you feel compelled to join me on this quest for *who knows what*.

"I don't think it a sin, I begin in answer to your anticipated question, to expect to see a unicorn or night hawk between the shadows of the redwoods who stand and watch."

NATURE MYTH

In the last days, as the night slowly descends on the human drama, love will bring rest to the tired soul, warming the frail, shivering frame on the coldest night of winter. In the last days, as the air becomes too heavy to breathe, hope will cease to float like a dream or any other unseen, unrequited pledge in the roaring westerly winds of May, or storm gusts through falling October leaves. It will descend into our lungs and exhale songs and psalms of joy.

In the last days, joy will rush out to greet the world like twelve excited apostles at Pentecost with a message of love and hope that only willing ears will hear. That the truth, after all this time, was indeed reflected in the myth of nature.

Then in these days, myth will cease to exist in the past as primitive answers to our fears as the stones will cry out "have you not read, have you not heard?!" in the presence of an unwilling audience. And as they run to find cover beneath these lively stones, they will know that the poets and prophets did indeed eat at the Master's table.

"My youth come to mind like a dream or more rather a movie playing in a crowded theater."

LIFE LIKE A MOVIE

When I reflect back on my life, what happened to me often does seem more like a movie I've watched rather than something I've experienced. There is a certain detachment I feel about my experiences, especially the good ones that feel tainted by the bad experiences that loom so much larger and consequently feel more "real." They're not any more real, of course, than the good ones but for some reason the bad experiences have a way of lingering on in my heart.

Life may be like a movie in the sense that our lives certainly play out like stories. In fact, they are stories, stories that are lived and experienced in the present moment. We are both the authors and the actors in our stories, so in some sense we can control our present story lines, but we don't have any editorial control over our past experiences, scenes, and chapters.

I think the analogy of being an actor in a story is a helpful one. It helps us to remember that we have a role to play not only in our own personal stories but also in the larger story we've been placed into. As actors in this story we can learn from our past, to both regret and rejoice in it, but we can also relish in the fact that the story continues no matter what has happened earlier.

I don't have to bury the past because it's a series of scenes that have qualified me to be here at this moment playing the role that I am and the role I will play in the future. It's an adventure. And yes, every adventure has those moments when all seems lost, but every adventure is a journey as well. And every journey is a moving forward toward something.

Since I've been running with a lot of analogies lately, I may as well continue. One of my favorite movies is "Braveheart," a story of heroism by a man who wished only for a simple life revolving around his first love and family. Early in the film, we find out that an outside evil had taken his father away from him at an early age and then years later, it takes his wife from him as well.

He becomes a hero when he defends his people against this evil instead of giving in to the temptation to live in the past and check out of his story. A terrible one at that, and yes, he does make the ultimate sacrifice in the end by giving up his life for his people. But he chose to reengage in his story and have an important say in the outcome of the bigger story around him.

Most of our lives will not have this kind of story arc, but I still reflect on the former scenes in my story, and I realize there is a lot more story left to be told. And now the tinge of depression I was feeling takes a backseat to the reality that this is still my story to tell, and I do, by the grace of God, have a say in how it will be written. I also have an advocate telling a larger one, who has my back through it all.

One last analogy. I'm reminded here of watching reruns of old serials that originally ran in movie theaters back in the 1940s-50s. At the end of each episode, which often involved a harrowing cliff hanger, the words "to be continued" filled the screen. In other words, "it may look hopeless now but it ain't over yet," and in the back of our minds we know good always wins in the end no matter how many cliff hangers we have to endure. As a believer, I have the assurance that the story of my life will end in victory, which means being united with all who have fought with me through the ages with our Author and Advocate even if all seems lost in the short run.

GOD IS MERCY

Today. This evening, I wonder at the words of Martin Luther, who cried out in surprise and joy when he first unlocked the truth, "God must be mercy, God is mercy!"

"Yes, God is mercy," whispers an eternal breeze blowing through walls and souls so quiet and easily one can miss it. If the will of God is unstoppable and Jesus came to set the prisoners free and our captivity is sin and death and the will of God is supreme, then "God is Love" must be some thing unbreakable.

Just what did he do for those three days underneath the as of yet unrolled away stone? He did not ascend to the Father, that came later. He did not go to Starbucks for coffee.

If to obey the command to relax rests on the grand notion that "the truth will be preached to all prisoners, " then can we not believe all the legalists wrong? New Pharisees return to the law like a dog returns to its vomit, and forget that Christ died to kill sin and death once and for all. And yet, I sit here questioning the mercy of God. No, not questioning maybe more asking for justification, which of course, I want on my terms.

"God loves me, but he doesn't like me." I don't think it's my voice, even though it sounds familiar, that repeats these lines over and over at the most inopportune times.

"When I am weak, he is strong." At this moment, I think I know what this phrase means. When I feel most weak in spirit when my flesh aches to be held, to be caressed and comforted, I'm often overtaken with a warmth flowing over me that I can't explain. A supernatural warmth that comforts as if unseen arms sense the cold wind of descent and slumber, encouraging me to embrace despair.

It feels like a sort of holy invasion. Not like the wages of sin are death but like gift of God is grace, not eternal sleep but eternal life, not like God is hate like the New Pharisees tell me but like God is love like holy men tell me over and over that "God is mercy."

GOING HOME TO MOVE FORWARD

A month ago, I decided to go home. A lot of us do that at some point in our lives. I'm sure a psychologist somewhere has called it "the Prodigal Son Syndrome." An irresistible pull toward familiar surroundings from a more simple time and the family and friends that we grew up with but left behind for greener pastures.

I think that definitely played a part in the decision. And from a career standpoint, well, there was no career worth pursuing anyway, so why not go home? Being around family and old friends has lived up to its billing, and I'm certainly glad that I did, though I have no idea how long this time will last.

The line I wrote above reminded me of a conversation I had with a friend just before I left to return home. I wasn't going home to find myself. I know who I am. I wasn't giving up, either, which was a reason I hadn't moved home earlier. It felt like a step I needed to take. I remembered a song, which had a line that went something like this, "sometimes going home feels like moving on."

The conversation got me to think a little deeper. I originally left Kansas from Nashville coming off an amazing period of restored faith and covering provided by the grace of God. What I didn't know at the time was that I was naive and unready for the challenges I was about to endure. "I've been through the wars and have the scars to prove it."

I know who I am and I know who I need to be, the adult version of the kid who left for Nashville wanting to make the world a better place. I'm less sure now of what I've been called to accomplish, but at least I know who I've been called to be. I don't now what will come in the future, but my faith remains strong, and I can rest, yes rest, assured "that they who wait for the Lord will renew their strength (Is. 40:31)."

NOTHING OTHER

In the quietest of moments, when the music stays content to remain in the next room, the air is filled with the voice of God. Praise is an act of volition set against the sedentary mass of emotionless creatures. I will, I will the praise of You to rise from my heart to lips to the ears of others. My song, as I am able to sing it, fights through the thick of an angry forest. It waters the trees starving for rest in the storm we all feel if not recognize.

The wind is You, the joy out of nowhere singing words that bring both peace and rest. In the surprising days of winter, the warm, southwesterly winds melt my frozen tears, and I'm able to feel Your love again in the loneliness of my spiritual December blizzard.

Winter stayed much longer and stronger than usual this year until sucker punched out the door by an early summer wind. Lord, sometimes I feel like a boat tossed about by the two warring sides of the sea. I'm too cold then too hot, not in one place long enough to feel settled. Yet, You are the North Star that shines between the at odds storm clouds.

The wind is You, the breeze I feel this midsummer Sunday afternoon, cooling the sweat rushing down the back of my neck. Rest and peace, weapons set against strongholds built between You, Lord, and Man. This land is not lost as long as the wheat strains its shocks up toward the heavens for something more, the joy that comes from being filled by the wind and the raining down of Your love from above.

The wind is You, every shade of cool and hot. The wind is You, every brush of breeze or gust, and I, sitting here, sort of sweating but not quite, breathing in/ breathing out nothing other than You.

THE BRIEF INTERLUDE

I'm at a turning point, or a moving forward point. The book I've been writing based on this blog is nearly finished. Fitting, because I'm back in Kansas and my life feels a little like summer break before the final semester of college begins. At some point soon, I'll be moving on and hopefully, I'll be prepared for whatever comes next.

Sure, I was young, excited, and unafraid, but I was unprepared. Nobody told me that my grace period would end. Satan knew I would be alone when I left for Nashville and bigger things, and more importantly, that I had areas of weakness that could be exploited. And boy, did this kid get exploited!

It's a typically hot (102 degree) day in July in Kansas. The fall is coming but it's still a few months off. For now, the heat will be reason enough to sit inside bedrooms and coffeehouses gazing outside at the full green leafed, wind blown tree limbs. Time doesn't stop, of course, even though the heat sustained by the rough, southerly winds tires the body while encouraging sleep or reflection.

I've lost a lot in the last five years, my career, my house, my savings, my retirement but not my faith. I'm past the point of wondering whether I'm being punished for some unknown sin. This is life. This is *my* life. The man sitting here just inside the window of a Topeka coffeehouse is indeed older and wiser than the younger man who left to take on the world years ago.

This is life. The brief interlude will end, and I will move forward into the next phase with all its trials and opportunities. I want to be ready for two things, whatever I'm called to do, and also prepared to move forward with a sober recognition of my weaknesses. I will not be played again by either life or evil.

Yes, this brief interlude is a chance to rest and lick my wounds, but if I'm not stronger when I return to the war than when I originally entered it, I will be no better off. I must get stronger, stronger than I have ever been before. Fortunately, now I know how. Keep in the Word, keep being grateful, even when I don't necessarily feel it, pray, and put others ahead of myself. A game plan for withstanding trials but more than that, succeeding for myself and others in the name of a God who stuck with me throughout it all and will continue to do so no matter how well or bad I do at any given moment.

THE RAIN OF PRAISE

Lord, the rest you offer me requires a quiet mind because the Whispering Genius will not strain his voice. In this instance, the peace inside my quietness sings a song of praise lifted up from within the closet, which is the innermost chamber of my heart.

Fly, my praise, out of my heart and into the air stale with the stench of centuries of man made sin. Angels will carry it through the sulfur tinged clouds up past the God made storm clouds and out into the quiet of space where it will finally join with the collected eternity of worship in the skies of New Jerusalem approaching.

Rest, heart,

the Whispering Genius, who lives within you, will teach you how to sing out to the Storm- King. His clouds above will rain down the praises you learn to help heal the wounded warriors of Christ.

Lord, I can hear the rain as it falls down on me, singing, "you are not alone, you are not alone," drop by drop as they cool my head hot from the kiln- fired air I breathe. Cool me, refresh me with the love my brothers and sisters share with their neighbors.

Sing, heart, the love you sing up to the storming skies will return to the earth, in turn, with the praise of others to bring rest and peace, quenching the fires of spiritual warfare to those who thirst for the strength to fight another day.

"The clock is ticking."

THE RIGHT NOW

"The summer, with all its tornadoes and sunbathing, demands all eyes on the thrill of the *right now*. Right now, I think there's nothing sexier than ponytails and tank tops worn by the right girl. If she were with me, as I leaned over the balcony rail fifty feet from the coast line, sharing a glass of white wine and moonlight, time would step aside and let my heart slow dance with hers as we shared the silence only love can bring."

I'm having to catch myself these past few days. By writing "The Brief Interlude," I was officially declaring the end of one phase in my life, which means the next phase should begin. Right now. The problem,though, is that I don't want to force it, lest the next phase becomes the wrong one, and I've wasted valuable time. I'm not 25 anymore. The clock is ticking. J's return is much nearer now, and I best be about the business at hand.

Meanwhile, the lunchtime coffeehouse air is buzzing with the quiet din of multiple conversations. Much like the bees who saved my Cherry Blossom tree last year, the white noise of conversationalists reminds me that there is an intentionality about creation. I'm not just here, I'm here for a reason. That should make me feel better except for the fact that, on many days, I allow myself to become paralyzed by stress. How can I be effective if I don't explicitly now what role I am to play?

I like to write stories, and one thing I know about writing stories is that as the author, I'm the one who assigns the roles to be played and how they will be played out. I know the end of the game. The actors in the story don't, they are living out their parts to the best of their abilities, always surprising me along the way with how they deal with the situations I place them in. I can learn something from them and the way they handle themselves. They aren't stressed about their roles, they're playing them out by being engaged in the story, the moment.

Right now, I know I'm in enemy occupied territory, and I have to keep focused on what's in front of me lest the antagonist win and the drama becomes a tragedy. The role I am to play, the "big picture role" I sweat over, will come to me. How I play it out in the meantime is up to me. To put it in simple terms, I have to be myself and let the rest come to me.

My character description reads something like this, "Christian guy whose life revolves around J. Not young but not yet old, either. Medium build. Likes to read, watch Jayhawk basketball, and can be quite the smart alack at times. He recognizes the war he's been placed in and counts on J to help him through it."

Right now, I want to spend time with my friend, J, who has the patience I aspire to and loves his creation in a way I desire to, and has the strength that I need to face the war with anger when it's required and humor when that's the more appropriate weapon. It's a Friday afternoon and what started out as a feeling of helplessness and impatience has turned into a moment of rest. Clarity has that effect.

Lord, help me to run the race with open eyes, ears that hear, and a willing heart, so I can surprise the enemy with my heart, resilience, and annoying habit of overcoming his plans through you.

MOST HIGH

You are the most high, Triune God, the lovely mystery solved within three persons, Father, Son, and Holy Spirit. You are the author of the salvation that we cling to when the condemning rains pour over our hair and skin.

You are the author of creation, whose breath spoke the first words of poetry ever written, "Let there be light." No wonder you are the light of the world then and now, piercing through the darkness of the sin filled air.

You are the light we will bask in as we walk the halls of the temple in New Jerusalem, and the pleasant green fields outside the city that will never see the darkness that currently consumes us. Lord, we wait breathlessly for the sunrise that will never end, the mountaintops that will never see bloodshed.

Meanwhile, Father, be the source of our ability to love, Son be the way through the valley of the shadow of death, and Spirit be the truth that sets us free. The one hope that thrives in the living temples walking about in the garden we currently call our world. You are the strength residing in us that allows us to confess, despite our weaknesses and our ever ready enemies, that Jesus Christ is the Lord over all and savior of our souls.

"Stumble as I may in my weaknesses, the hand of my Friend is still there to lift me up again."

J'S LOVE BREAKING THROUGH

"Like a foolish dreamer trying to build a highway to the sky/ All my hopes would come tumbling down/ And I never knew just why/ Until today, when you pulled away the clouds/ That hung like curtains on my eyes."

"Your Love Broke Through"— Keith Green

I first heard this song in my studio apartment just after I moved to Nashville. After rediscovering my faith while at Kansas University, I went through a period of renewing my relationship with Christ. It didn't affect my life much at first, but as time went by, everything began to change. My former life suddenly felt like a dark dream one day when I'd finished jogging through campus. I was looking around the north edge of the campus on my right and the neighborhood apartments on my left, and every color became dazzling like someone had upgraded my senses from analogue to High Definition television. It was extraordinary!

Of course, my senses became accustomed, or used to, this new clarity but it was the beginning of a peace that lasted mostly uninterrupted for the rest of my time at the university. The opening lines to the song listed above hit me hard, and I nearly cried with joy when I heard them. "Real life" hadn't hit me just yet, but the music and lyrics took me back to that day when my perspective on life suddenly changed.

Many years have passed since I first heard Keith Green's beautiful song, and I had quite frankly forgot about it until this evening when it found its way out of my Ipod and into the air while I was reading. Could it be a coincidence that I heard this song at a time when I'm beginning to regain some of that childlike faith I had when I first heard it so long ago? Maybe. Still, that gratefulness Green sings about in this song remains relevant in my life. Especially now when my heart is yearning for that relationship I had back in those days of regained innocence.

The good news is that even a war torn spirit can still feel that presence, that peace that surpasses understanding. It comes with an earnest desire for the presence of God. Often, the scars run so deep that the peace doesn't last for long. War wounds will continue to be ripped open by the Enemy that gave them in the first place until the conflict has finally ceased forever. That's the nature of the war I find myself in. Fortunately, the healing J brings is the foe of death and injury.

The better news is that the healing I'm seeking, the peace that comes from the presence of the Holy Spirit, literally comes from a higher power. The writer of the "Serenity Prayer" was on to something. The love of God does indeed break through and the peace, though often fleeting, keeps returning to heal the wounds that have built up during the course of the war we call real life.

Today, the song that made me nearly cry when I first heard it, reminds me that that peace that comes with his presence, still more my relationship with him, continues to be real despite the artillery shells being hurled at it. The accumulated wounds still hurt, but I'm reminded, again, that they're not fatal. Stumble as I may in my weaknesses, the hand of my Friend is still there to lift me up again. His love breaks through the Enemy's lines, not just once but every day the battle continues to rage on, and there are moments when the clouds of mortar shells part, and I can see more clearly.

MY OLD FRIEND

"To be born again means not the act of reentering your tired old mother's blood stained womb. That is nothing, but to be born again, truly, with eyes wide open, this is everything. And nothing short of eternity's gate will wash away the rolling, angry clouds.

I stopped running, not a metaphorical run, just jogging down 12th Street, just north of blue, gray Memorial Stadium where we, the faithful, unhopeful spent Saturdays in September, October, November dutifully watching the losses pile high with the dead and falling green, red, and brown leaves on the well groomed, well painted artificial grass.

I stopped because the jog was over. I did not see the clouds roll away, yet the veil lifted just the same. Nature's clouds remained, whiter than they'd been in years. The blue brilliant, hurting my eyes, exciting my senses. Yes, at that time I stood amazed, well more happy within the clarity of the moment.

An old friend descended between the white pillars. He would not talk to me at that moment, the moment of his descending, only smiling and nodding at those angels and spirits descending or ascending respectively.

"Why do angels only descend?," I asked. He only smiled. He would not talk openly of such things. But he would walk. And he would listen. And he would smile.

Looking back at the days I would one day write the above opening to in a short story based loosely on my life,

I remember that J often felt as much like a friend, and fellow traveler, as my Lord and Savior. It was during this period that the poster signed "With love, J" hung on my apartment wall (see Appendix). That's not as crazy as it might initially sound, that of J being a friend. He refers to his disciples as friends during the Last Supper in the Gospel of John. Surely the disciples felt at once comforted and honored by this. What if one of the ways that our God comes to us is as a friend?

In many ways over the years, I've let that relationship slip in the sense of that kind of intimacy that comes with friendship. I need J to be my savior now more than ever, but the peace that came from our friendship is something I want as well. Lately, I've felt the tugging of my heart to return to those days. I can't return to those days, of course, but like reconnecting with old friends from the past, I can reconnect with my "old friend" in much the same manner.

Old friendships renewed bring new memories, that while not the same as the early ones, are just as real, and in this sense, you can go home again. The joy that arose from connecting with old friends and kindred spirits still exists despite all the years and distance that have been traveled. I'm still walking the path I've been placed on, making mistakes, getting frustrated with myself and the world around me, but I'm still moving forward. And if I allow J to be both friend as well as Lord, then I think the wilderness, with all the trials and tribulations it will continue to throw at me, will not have the power to make me lose sight of the hope that can't be taken away from me. Nor can it take away from me anyone I choose to call friend.

THE JOURNEY'S NOT OVER

I'm on my way now. Like the storm clouds that enter ominously in from western Kansas in the hot afternoons of August, the future looms with a similar aura of danger and mystery. The thing about storm clouds, though, is that there is a sort of majesty as well as mystery about them if I choose to look at them through the lens of my faith, my strength.

If I face them without fear, standing, waiting, and watching as the spectacular, powerful arctic rush of the wind that precedes them cools skin hot from a long summer, it becomes a future I can look forward to. If I'm lucky, they will try to knock me over, blast after blast, as I watch the approaching darkness rush over me, the pitch black of the clouds shaking with thunderclaps and lightning streaking side to side through the barely visible openings between them. It's fun, dare I offer, to face the fear head on.

I'm on my way now more conscious of the fact that I'm not alone. I'm allowing my friend to be a friend again and the danger lying ahead, whatever it may be, looks less imposing. This is not the end to my journey. Far from it. I don't have all of the answers and how many I have I'm not really sure. But a veil has lifted, lifted again I should say.

After all these months, first acknowledging the fact that evil is set against me, and secondly, my right to the abundant life J has not only offered to me but fights for me to have, has helped me to better understand the war I'm in the middle of. An active evil has been fighting me all along under the guise of hopelessness and the heaviness of denial and apathy. Not that I haven't made a lot of mistakes along the way, I have, but realizing my place in the story and, to a better extent, the other characters in it, helps me to understand a little better what's going on.

Recognizing the Apathy monster for what it is and shrugging it off hasn't proven to be easy. But the journey through the wilderness has given me a great deal of perspective on the story I find myself in. Faith and the war that comes with it. It won't end until the Author (J) steps onto the stage, bringing with him the end to all the pain and struggles we often call real life.

Meanwhile, the journey continues on and the lessons I've learned will walk with me into the next scene that I find myself in and the ones after that. The journey continues with all the mystery, danger, excitement, and yes, anticipation that comes with living in an adventure story. In the midst of the darkest hour, the moment in the story when it seems all is lost, a path to victory has been found and the enemy, while still powerful, and as of yet not defeated, sees the tide is turning, and knowing the time is short, will lash out with all the anger and intimidation it can muster. What lies ahead is the march forward toward the distant kingdom, which all the while, approaches its heroes.

Until that day, as Lewis once said, "the cross comes before the crown." The happy ending, while inevitable, is a way off yet, perhaps a long way off. The good news is that this life is a journey and that means it's either a path to be tread with heads down or an adventure to be embraced with expectant heads held high.

EMERGING FROM THE SHADOWS

I was going to title this blog *2014: The War In Review*. But I just finished reading the chapter on evil from Ravi Zacharias' book *Jesus Among Other Gods,* and I'm thinking a little bit more of the big picture of my experiences over the past several years. One of the things I've been thinking about since I have emerged from the shadows (more on that in a moment) is something I've talked with friends about. That is, you can never really know why you are going through a trial or what you are supposed to learn from it until after you have come out of it. Six months later, I'm still wondering.

From the start, I should mention that bitterness is not a part of the equation anymore. Jesus has healed that wound in me, and it's a large part of how I was able to emerge at all. Looking back, it was a gradual change in how I approached God on a day to day basis. I first rededicated myself to immersing myself in the Bible and the study of theology, two things that have helped me to grow as a person and stay focused on the things that matter. Second, I decided to live a life of gratitude, which meant thanking God each morning for the day, whether I was really feeling grateful for it or not. For me, that has become a way for me to throw a punch at evil before it has a chance to strike me.

The boxing metaphor might seem a little strange, but I can't think of a single day in my life where I haven't been challenged by something or someone. It could be something as small as someone cutting me off in traffic and my response to it or something bigger like having my pay cut by 25 percent and then having a job I held for eleven years suddenly ending. Peter calls Satan a lion prowling around looking for someone to devour. Look at your daily life, doesn't it seem like something or someone is constantly trying to undercut your happiness, and by extension, your faith?

That is why I titled my blog *Christianity Is A War*, because evil, life, or whatever you want to call it, is trying to take our joy away from us. Because if it can do that, it can move on to taking away the joy we have in Christ and then it's on to our very faith. This is serious stuff going on here. We are at war. We can choose to ignore evil but obviously it is not ignoring us.

Back to the shadows. August of 2014 was the breakthrough month for me. I was back in Kansas enjoying my time around my parents, my sister, her kids, and the friends I grew up with, while trying to figure out my next move. I was still struggling financially along with all the other issues I was dealing with, but I was home and moving back (in June) was one of the best decisions I have made in a long time. If you get the chance, go back and reread my blog *Going Home To Move Forward*.

I emerged from the shadows, because I changed my mindset, and that mindset first rewarded me with peace, the peace that Paul calls "the peace that passes all understanding (Phil 4:7)." At that point, I was still two months away from getting offered a good job, and I could not have pointed to any material thing that made me feel like I was emerging from what felt like a life with no hope. Yet, here I was feeling the peace of God and wondering where eight years of bitterness went.

All is not sunshine and roses, of course. I still have scars (material, physical, emotional, and to some extent spiritual) that are in the long process of healing. But the healing has begun, I believe, because I made the decision to pursue a closer relationship with Jesus and took the stubborn position of being grateful even though I didn't feel like there was a reason to be grateful. One last thought, as the bitterness disappeared, I began to thank God for every good thing that happened to me, no matter how small a thing it might seem to be, and the peace I didn't see coming has remained always nearby.

APPENDIX: J'S COMING, LOOK BUSY!

There is a certain kind of temptation. It's a tricky one that sneaks up on us when we're feeling particularly righteous or religious. But it can't be a temptation because it feels good. It can't be wrong if it feels good, right? Is it really a temptation if we're sure God wants us to give in to it? The temptation we seem to think God wants us to give in to is *seriousness*.

Have you fallen for this one? Here is a quick test, I saw a tee shirt once that said, "Jesus is coming. Look busy!" Did you laugh or duck for fear of a lightning strike? I'm not going where you think with this. I personally think the tee shirt is funny, though, yeah, when Jesus returns we "best be about the business." If you've been following this blog for any time at all, you know that I often refer to him as "J." It may have struck you as odd or even blasphemous. At the very least, disrespectful, but I have a very good reason for doing it here. Jesus isn't just my Lord and Savior, though that is quite enough, he's also my friend. The one I want to walk with on this journey through what often feels like enemy occupied territory.

"J" has a story, though. Early in my last year at Kansas University, I found a rather poignant poster of a pencil drawing of Jesus. In this drawing/poster Jesus is looking at us with a smile that merely says "I love you." What made this poster even more endearing to me was that it was signed in big letters like on a post card we might send from the beach to loved ones,

With love,

J

That's part of what I'm thinking here when I refer to Jesus as "J" in this blog, now book. I have a savior that loves me as I am. But there's more to it than that, J has many names for a reason, and that reason is that he really is all things to all people at all times, including friend.

THE MANY NAMES OF GOD

I AM. Jehovah. Messiah. Christ. Jesus.
   The First and the Last. Father. Lord.
   Author and finisher of our Faith.
   We read about I AM and Jehovah
   the way we read Tolstoy and Dostoyevsky.
   We anticipate Messiah
   along with all lost and yearning souls.
   Christ saved and continues to save our souls.
   And to say "Jesus" brings out love or hatred
   or any other feeling in between
   except for apathy or complacency.
   The First and the Last,
   or Alpha and Omega for those into Greek,
   pretty much covers it all.
   And doesn't He cover it all?
   Father with open arms, Lord who bends the knees,
   and Finisher who lifts us up again.
   But what about Friend?
   Who walks with us, lays down his life for us?
   Who would give so much more to us,
   if only to hear us call him,
   among the many other names, Friend.

Printed in the United States
By Bookmasters